I0196788

Thought provoking and alluring, 9 4 will take you on a spiraling journey starting in the palms of your hands and ending in love, with both the characters and story, leaving you with a craved desire for the next addicting read.

The journey traveled within 9 4 is one for the imagination, equipped with every human emotion possible. (The Introduction) allows beautiful emotion driven intimate poetry. (Dark Twisted Love Tales) offers all the many sides of love, following four stories closely as each risks it all for love, only to suffer the fears; abandonment, defeat, heartbreak, power, innocence, pain. (Dark Twisted Love Tales) are indeed dark and twisted, in this case good prevails. (Words To Live By, Me) redirects the darkness into a positive, motivating section where you'll find thoroughly thought out quotes, with inspiring words to live by. (Daisy) is most interesting, a perfect reminder that life is full of uncertainties and in the end, there is love and there is hope, which is equivalent to beauty.

9 4 is more than a poetry book, to name it fairly would be "A storybook with poetry as its narrator." It is demanding, captivating, sensual, and empowering, heart warming, heart breaking, and exciting. M. Randall has found a language that speaks fluently to all, Introducing the breathtaking 9 4, Enjoy the ride.

9 4

THE INTRODUCTION

M. RANDALL

Copyright © 2014 by M. Randall

"This is for the believers, Thank you for believing in me.

CONTENTS

THE INTRODUCTION	
VIRGO	2
I AM, EVERYTHING	3
HEART OF GOLD	4
I HATE	5
DENSE	6
ALL RIGHTS RESERVED	7
BEAUTY OF ESSENSE	8
SEASONS	9
SHINE	10
7DAY, FORECAST	12
CAUGHT IN THE MIDDLE	13
DANCE TO THE MOON	14
FREE	15
SHADOWS	16
WHAT HURTS THE MOST	17
BURNING LETTERS, BY	18
THE VISITOR	19
BUT, I WISH YOU HAPPINESS	20
I AM, MIRROR	22
DARK TWISTED LOVE TALES	
THE CROWN	23

SERPENT	24
TO BE KING	26
ROYAL BLOOD	27
ROYAL BLOOD, SPILLED	29
BEHEADING OF THE KING	31
I AM, QUEEN	33
LONG LIVED THE KING	34
THE SWORD	35
WORDS AS WEAPONS	36
RED DRESS	38
THE SUITOR, WHO KNEW	42
PERFUME	43
PRINCESS, FAIRY, OR GYPSY	44
TWO WORLDS, APART	45
JEZEBEL	46
SUB DIVISION	47
FLAWLESS STARS	48
THE CROSS	49
DARKNESS	50
SORROWED LONGING	51
MAGICAL FOREST	52
COUSIN	53
FORBIDDEN LOVE	54
SAVE YOURSELF	56

RUN	57
THIEF	58
OBJECTIONS	60
THE LAST LETTER	62
ENDS IN LOVE	64
WORDS TO LIVE BY, ME	
MADNESS, PRAYER	65
TIME	66
FADED	67
THE PAST	68
FREEDOM	69
EAGLE	70
SING, GLEAM, BEAM	71
AFRAID	72
NATURE	73
GOOD MUSIC	74
ANCHORS	75
NEW PEOPLE	76
BLINDING LIGHT	77
HOPE	78
INFINITE	79
BELIEVE IN THYSELF	80
DAISY	
COFFEE SHOP	82

OH, DAISY	84
GHOST OF A SMILE	87
GOODBYE, JUNE	88
PERFECT	89
94	90

THE INTRODUCTION

VIRGO

It's more about

The way I comprehend.

My voice of reason,

Relating well with others.

The way I over analyze almost

Everything.

It's my chameleon soul.

The gentleness in my approach,

I take pleasure in pleasing.

I seemingly have the world sorted out,

Keeping secrete

The worries and doubts.

I'll cry for you before myself,

I pray for the world.

I am a hopeless romantic.

I'm an introvert,

Naturally reluctant.

I both,

Love and hate my flaws.

It's the way I find beauty in most things

Overall.

I've been called a perfectionist

For my hard working ethic,

Virgo,

Oh

Virgo,

There is madness in your methods.

I AM EVERYTHING

I Am

A warrior,

Fighting with a furious rage.

I Am

A soldier

On the front line,

Pin-pilling the grenade.

I Am

A leader

Leading the free world.

I believe in me,

I believe in you.

I Am

Youth

Awaiting my blossom.

I Am Everything

Because,

Anything is possible.

HEART OF GOLD

I don't think that I'm faster,

Smarter,

Or better.

I just feel,

I think differently.

I find life to be indeed full of beauty

Well,

Not always,

But!

We have the freedom to choose,

Choose happiness

Every day,

Every minute,

Every second.

Be you,

Be *free*.

I HATE

I Hate

The way

I get self conscious about the smallest of things

Or how,

I love to be recognized

But hate the attention.

I Hate

When I meet someone for the first time

And my nerves force my words in either direction.

I Hate

The way, I

Always,

Never feel comfortable in my clothes.

I Hate,

That

I Hate,

What

I Hate

Most.

DENSE

I operate on the morality of truth,

I speak volume into those who choose.

I wish not to pretend

Things are all figured out,

I've vowed to never,

Not,

Figure it out.

ALL RIGHTS RESERVED

I have the *Right*

To be heard.

I have the *Right*

To fly amongst the birds.

I have the *Right*

To be the person I am,

I posses the *Right*

To win.

I have the *Right*

To encourage a friend.

I have the *Right*

To live as an Eagle,

Free as a bird.

I have the *Right*

To speak efficiently

With authority within my words,

I will be heard.

All Rights Reserved.

BEAUTY OF ESSENCE

There's grace in the softness of your touch,

A calming gentleness in your

"I Love you so much."

Peace in your presence,

You are indeed

Beauty

And all of its

Essence.

SEASONS

Let there be smiles

In the winter,

Laughter in *June*,

A goodbye that came all too soon.

Allow summer to shine down

Finding its way upon you.

When the leaves fall

In November, remember

All there is to remember.

Christmas comes fast,

Find me underneath the mistletoe.

Halloween is ominous,

Good thing I have your hand to hold.

Autumn just passes,

I allow it to.

Spring is warm,

Bringing sunshine when skies are blue.

Seasons, oh *Seasons*,

I'd travel them for you.

SHINE

Let the rain fall,

Bestowing joy upon you,

Let the nightfall see you home.

Let love be your guiding light,

The one you count on.

7DAY, FORECAST

Monday brought on rain,

Tuesday the same.

The weather storms

With displeasure,

Whenever

That you leave.

Wednesday welcomes snow,

Thick white fluff pour down.

Thursday the wind is aggressive

Swirling my week around.

By Friday there's now

Rain, snow, and wind,

Friday, was Friday,

Rain, snow, and wind.

Friday, sly Friday,

Hiding the tornado within.

Saturday begin thundering and lightening too,

Roaring so loud

Indeed a frightening view.

On Sunday you returned along with the sun,

I rejoice for the moment

Before you could run.

Thank you dear Sunday,

Always retrieving my Sun.

CAUGHT IN THE MIDDLE

When you've made up your mind

Then, changed it just in time.

Caught In The Middle

That moment your heart says wait

Then, you proceed anyway.

Caught In The Middle

The second your body refused to move,

Caught In The Middle

With nothing to lose, still

Caught In The Middle

I'd suggest you choose.

DANCE ME TO THE MOON

I loved you in May,

We met in April,

Danced in

June.

You cried in July,

Or May,

Or maybe it was

June.

I do remember us

However,

Dancing To The Moon.

FREE

I fought not only for you,

Also For me.

I fought for the chance

That one day we'd be

Free.

SHADOWS

Seeing your face

Regardless of what I do,

Lately

In my dreams

The only way of viewing you

Close my eyes

And there you are.

Dreaming of you,

Where ever you are.

Before you were sent to me

Then,

Incomplete.

Sometimes it rained

Leaving deep puddles,

Whenever I'd looked closely,

You were there,

Always in the *Shadows*.

WHAT HURTS THE MOST

This was far more than a simple crush,

It happened the way you

Fall, fall, fall in love.

When I close my eyes I still see you,

When the wind blows,

I still breath you.

Even when I'm dreaming,

Only then I find

Your heart is never fleeing.

Reality

It's impossible to hold a heart

Infamous for leaving.

Closing my eyes for another dose,

Remembering they must reopen is

What Hurts The Most.

BURNING LETTERS, BY

By

My bed for you,

I've lit them a flame

Hoping the message finds you.

Burnings Letters, By

The ocean side,

It's the only place my tears can hide.

Burning Letters, By

The fireplace,

Perhaps the black smoke would be able to explain

The tears upon my face

Burning Letters, By

Gas stations,

Hoping the fuel would have the explanation.

Burning letters, By

My bedside,

Here for you.

I've read them time again,

I *burn* them freeing myself of you.

THE VISITOR

I came only for a short while,

Knowing you not

Anymore.

I came all this way

Just to see

If the love you had

Is still there for me.

Counting my ducats,

Sowing them where they may.

I came all this way

Just to see,

If our love still exists today.

BUT, I WISH YOU HAPPINESS

If my space has been replaced,

In my honor,

Let it have brought a smile to your face.

If the heart I had once known

Suddenly overgrown,

Let there be strength enough to carry on.

If the hand meant for me to hold

Somehow became cold,

Please give it a warmer,

Softer

Hand to hold.

I AM, MIRROR

You gaze into my soul every day

Yet,

Never do you stop and say

"Mirror,

How is your day?"

Or,

"Thank you mirror for displaying such exquisite perfection."

I have memorized your flaws,

Even when you cry,

I know you best

Yet,

Never do you ever

Second-guess,

To check in on me

Or view what I see.

I cried today

Unselfishly for you,

Even with all of your perfect sight,

And outwardly vanity,

You are still

Without a clue.

Staring at me each day,

Refusing to see you.

DARK TWISTED LOVES TALES

THE CROWN

An ornamental circlet head covering made of iron, gold, metal and fairy dust, stained with both Serpent's venom and blood. Worn by the most high, King, Queen or empire of a monarch. The power position, symbolizing wealth, power, and greed. Many armies have fallen short of its glory, only to drown in the fury of the beloved CROWN. Blessed be the soul it is bestowed upon.

SERPENT

I danced a *Serpent*

In the dark,

I must admit

It wasn't smart.

I studied the bravery of the *Serpent*

Known for its brave heart.

A snake is a snake,

I knew the *Serpents*

Species from the start,

I often studied its sneaky ways.

For that is how I defeated the *Serpent*

In the dark days.

TO BE KING

With all royalty,

Even with my nobility

I could never be *King*

Suit me up in the finest of gold,

Garments, and armor,

Maids, servants and royals

Came to see the *King* to be.

Listening for a word,

I stood without one to speak.

I sunk as they stared,

Watching their wondering eyes.

No surprise

I could never be *King*

The crowd, they raved

Screamed for my reign,

Igniting the *Royal Blood*

Flowing through my veins,

Fueling them enough,

Turning a flame.

Today I am *King*

For I accept the offer,

Envision me on your throne

Ruling the parted seas.

I accept the throne,

For it belongs to me.

ROYAL BLOOD

Bow at the alter,

Freeing me of my sin.

I believe in the throne

In which I have come to seize,

I believe in the things belonging to me.

I believe in my crown

In which I've come to see,

Bring it at once,

Bow before me.

Show me my gold

Bring me a sword

The biggest there is to hold.

I am *King*, hear me roar.

My wrath is for my ancestors,

I am here to avenge our throne left behind,

I'm prepared to go to war for what's befittingly mine.

You are all under my powers,

I've come just in time.

I am *Royal Blood*

This throne is mine.

ROYAL BLOOD, SPILLED

I am, *Queen*

In which you have awakened.

My demons are released,

Protecting this castle

You've set your heart on overtaking.

This indeed may be where

Royal Blood, Spilled

But I'm afraid my dear,

Here you might be killed.

Alone, requesting my land.

I will exit your existence,

Now fitting you into my plans.

I am, Queen

Hear me roar,

I am prepared to battle,

Soldiers suited for War.

You speak of your ancient ancestors,

The greatness they've built.

What a pity,

I recall the lavish

Royal Blood, Spilled

I agree it was a horrifying sight,

So many were killed.

Back to the matter,

I am, Queen

Intrude me if you will

And your *Blood* too,

Will be *Spilled*.

BEHEADING OF THE KING

I'd stand on a mountain

Infested with territorial lions,

That would be foolish.

I'd give up my throne

Without denying

I'm a fool.

I'd part the ocean and seas for you

Even then,

I'm a fool.

How deep actually is this abyss?

Because if you're there

I wouldn't resist,

Such a fool for you.

Question existing,

What wouldn't I do?

Yes,

It's true,

I'm a fool.

Throw me out of a plane without my parachute,

Fly me to the *Moon*

Without oxygen,

Keep me there until I collapse.

Quite the fool,

Or just in love,

Perhaps.

Charge me right with the charge of the soul.

Lead me into *Darkness*,

Across a bridge,

To a place that no one knows.

Such a fool.

Take my words,

Use them against me.

With those same words,

I'll build walls for your protecting.

Drive a stake right through my heart,

Charge me with the charge of my heart.

Behead me for the sins of my heart

Even then, we shall never part.

Forgive me my *Queen*

You've intended only my head,

Successfully capturing my heart.

I AM, QUEEN

Tell me the things in which

Need be true.

Tell me the lies

Those "Ancestors told you."

Yes,

You've confessed your sparkle for me

I Am a ruler,

Queen

With immense duties,

I Am, Queen

Stand on the mountaintop

Infested with vicious lions,

You'd then be a precise target

For my hunters, gaming.

I do however,

Admire your dear admiration for me.

Oftentimes, I find

The position of power isn't the place to be.

Forgive me of my ill manners,

For you will never experience this magnitude of royalty.

Off with his head,

I Am, Queen

This *Royal* throne belongs to me!

LONG LIVED THE KING

"If *Blood* is to *Spill*

On behalf of my fathers,

Allow me to rejoice

Without further sorrows.

Free me of my head,

Place it over your throne.

Let it be your reminder,

That my

Royal Blood, Spilled

Too,

Here on this throne."

THE SWORD

A weapon cursed upon time, used verbally and or nonverbally. Typically identified as long, straight or curved blade, sharp-edged on one or both sides, and sits in a hilt. THE SWORD blades are of corruption, kissed with poison, cursed with death. Within THE SWORD, is of power and destruction for all things, both living and or nonliving. He, who perishes by THE SWORD, shall be casted into the place that exceeds both mortal, and immortal realms. It is there that he shall remain forever.

WORDS AS WEAPONS

Your *Words,*

They are delivered in such reproach,

Slicing like knives

Across the throat,

The blades are much more.

Using *Words,*

Hurt

Pierces the core.

Your *Words,*

And daggers are the same,

Master Assassinators.

Realizing

I was the blaming.

In that moment

I changed.

RED DRESS

Suitors in sight,

She danced alone for the night.

Forgetting the Princes

Who watched in awe.

She continued in her

Red Dress

Without a flaw,

Met all the royals,

Even shook hands.

Those dear Princes,

They didn't stand a chance.

She found it humorous how they fell to her glory,

Running out of time.

Thought,

She'd better hurry.

Midnight had come

Taking her away,

She danced for the moment,

Never minding the day.

Finally it had come,

That day was finally here.

Leaving behind the flowing

Red Dress

While she disappeared.

THE SUITOR, WHO KNEW

They lined up,

Princes from across the seas,

Eyes gleaming bright

Awaiting the mysterious girl they've come to meet.

She was said to appear

On the passing of decades of years,

Under a full *Moon*

Was she to disappear,

That only true loves kiss

Could keep her here.

There was a Prince,

Charming as can be

He too,

Known for his grace and beauty.

He in particular, aware of her

Dark dazzling secrete,

She must find true love,

Cast her spell,

Only then will she keep it.

She belonged to another world,

On another planet she was a goddess.

He waited with endless fascination,

Glancing around,

Noticing the other *Suitors*

Growing impatient.

Then, the announcement

"The Princess has arrived,"

Suitors

Straighten up protecting their titles.

It became clear,

She'd become an idol.

He fixed his eyes on the open grand staircase

She wore a *Red Dress,*

Moving with such gracefulness.

He recognized the alluring innocence in her eyes.

With much fascination he observed

As she made rounds, shaking hands,

Meeting Prince's from the different lands.

He knew soon she'd have to return,

But for now it's just her and the

Red Dress

Dancing to every song.

Suitors

Drew near in hopes of her hand,

Midnight was approaching,

Now was the chance.

Swiftly forcing his way through the crowd,

Past the others who spectated with astonishment

While he perused her.

She danced free in the night,

Understanding her power,

Love at first sight.

Holding his stare,

Their souls became one.

Now captive to her gaze,

He stood frozen as she changed,

Frozen he remained.

Midnight struck

And the girl disappeared.

The *Red Dress*

She leaves behind,

He pretends to be her,

When he wishes to be near.

The Suitor now sits alone

Wishing on *Stars*

Begging for faster years.

"I wish to be where you are."

He whispers

Praying for the answers in our

Flawless Stars.

PERFUME

Fresh cut flowers

In every room,

White sunlight

Ignites a bloom,

Creating an intoxicating blossom.

Smell as sweet as innocence,

Lingering the air with such magnetic perfection.

Your *Perfume,*

It's your most forbidden possession.

PRINCESS, FAIRY, OR GYPSY

I'm unsure of what you are,

Your creature forsakes me.

Princess, Fairy or Gypsy

Your eyes gleam mean,

Your hair breathes night.

Your skin is sun kissed,

Glowing a shimmering bright.

There is something in you,

A pulling force draws me.

What are you love,

Princess, Fairy, or Gypsy?

TWO WORLDS, APART

Life

Love

Death,

All with their limits.

Why hadn't you realized me sooner?

Only now is it,

 Time,

That prohibits.

Most things in which you see,

I am a victim of times captivity.

There's something inside you

That draws my soul across seas.

"Why must you soar nearest the *Moon?*

Stay here, cast your spell on me."

My world indeed,

Exists in a land unknown to you.

To stay only brings trouble,

They'd come seeking you.

Oh, how I wish to accept your offer,

I must go, for this is my final hour.

JEZEBEL

"Be free with the things you are

Free with."

He said.

"I think now is the time, my love.

It is my virtue you shall leave with."

She replied.

"I will allow you time,

Before your innocence is mine."

"The time is now,

It's all that we have.

The time is now,

Let's not let our time pass."

SUB DIVISION

Lost eternally

In both,

Love and addiction,

Faced with a choice,

Decision

After

Decision

United we stand,

Blurring our vision.

Press your sweet lips against mine love,

Before our *Sub Division*.

FLAWLESS STARS

Each night

I wish on millions of

Stars.

Wishing for brilliance,

I'd settle just to be where you are.

Until that day

I'll be wishing on

Stars.

THE CROSS

"There is no fear in love. But perfect love drives out fear, because fear has to do with punishment. The one who fears is not made perfect in love. We love because he first loved us."

1 JOHN 4:18-19

DARKNESS

Steadfast,

Hold on,

The *Darkness* is near,

Please be strong.

Silence the sniffles,

Silence the tears.

Deep down

I am nothing like you,

I belong to the monsters

And goblins, too.

I live and breathe under the moon

Darkness is here

It came all too soon.

SORROWED LONGING

I often long

For my place,

Where I belong.

I was an unusual child,

My heart running wild,

With a fire for every opportunity,

Addicted to each experience,

Birthing an invincible rage.

Still and now,

I search for my place.

MAGICAL FOREST

Down in the *Forest,*

Deep in the trees,

There is a

Magical Tale

Full of mystery,

Lurking in the air,

Lingering upon the leaves,

Down in the

Forest,

Deep in the trees,

There is *Magic* waiting for me.

COUSIN

Sleep is the

Cousin

To death.

We lay until we fall,

Fall until we fade.

When I lay

I go to the unknown.

FORBIDDEN LOVE

"My love,

Don't waste your tears.

For I belong in a world unknown here.

Heaven or Hell,

I will love you forever,

Immortal years.

Trust me love,

My truth will set you

Free.

Kiss it, my love.

Death,

Enjoy it with me."

SAVE YOURSELF

"Don't get too close,

There's *Darkness* Inside."

The boy said, pulling away.

"Well, It's my heart I can't deny."

She cried, taking a step closer

Extended her hands, welcoming his.

"You must run. Go away and hide.

I'm no good for you."

He shouted, pain filling every word,

Comforted with gentleness and delicacy.

It became obvious

He wished not to harm her,

Finding it to be the only way.

She lowered her head

Both,

Allowing and hiding the escaping tears.

"Without you,

I'm without a living purpose,

I'm wasting my years.

This forsaken world

Has no place in it for me without you,

Without you I shall not be.

I don't know where you belong,

But please, stay here with me.

Days without you, I wish not to see."

She managed through uncontrollable sobs.

His face tightens,

Jaws clinched together,

Watching silently as she drowned in sorrow,

Accompanied by misery.

Pain now upon the boys face,

He struggled with the exact emotion,

Turning a whiter shade of pale,

Eyes filled with regret.

Still he turned,

Running fiercely into the eerie silent forest.

She watched until his image disappeared into the

Darkness

Fading into only a memory.

RUN

It's the fluttering of butterflies,

Invading the pit of my stomach.

The constant voice saying

"You should be *Running*."

I stay when I know I should go,

My feet become complacent,

Refusing so.

THIEF

In silence you faded away,

The way a *Thief* does.

Your enforcing words enforced,

With such a passionate force.

Leaving on the still of the night,

We weren't to part.

As a *Thief* does,

Running through the *Darkness*

With my heart.

OBJECTIONS

When we met

I could sense trouble to be near.

Casting my fears aside,

I disobeyed.

My mind spoke obscenities,

Cursed in everyway.

My bones, they shivered,

Silent they remained.

My soul,

It drifted with fascinated curiosity.

My eyes closed tight,

Refusing to see.

My fingers they wouldn't grasp

Or connect with your grip.

Whenever we were close,

My lips refused your lips.

My heart found out all the

Objections

Deciding for itself,

The beauty in your imperfections.

Needless to say,

Loving any way,

Refusing *Objections*

Perhaps,

The reason I'm alone today.

THE LAST LETTER

As I stand on the edge of our fragile grounds

Holding the last piece of you,

A *Letter* I Found

Enclosed with your kiss.

In that moment,

I did it,

I begin to reminisce.

Quickly

Casting those memories aside,

Readjusting my posture,

Readjusting my pride.

It's a constant battle,

Remembering to forget.

Remember to forget,

I'm reminded.

Taking a step closer,

Inching toward the edge.

Pondering

Freeing myself of its ledge.

Instead

I crumple the sweet love *Letter*

Into a fist

The stabbing pain,

Again

This happens always,

Whenever I forget.

With a final breath,

I release my dearest love *Letter*.

I'm flushed with regret,

Keeping it may have been better.

ENDS IN LOVE

Locked away in the east wing of the dark intimidating castle,

Blizzard behaved snow finds its way through the black mountains,

Resting there,

Preparing to meet me at my great escape.

Afraid of what awaits.

Without second thought,

I make a run for it.

The guards,

They chase after me.

I

Run,

Run, Run

Finding myself barefooted in the thick white powder snow,

Each step buries me further,

Lost in the white forest with nowhere else to go.

Finally it happens,

The cold consumes me.

Falling frozen,

Instant chills and shivering.

I close my eyes to meet your face,

When you are near

I feel safe.

Even though,

I'm drifting into a space unknown to man,

I see your face

In my final hour

I envision us

Hand in hand.

_____*WORDS TO LIVE BY, ME*

MADNESS, PRAYER

"I cry when I think of the *Madness*

Of the world,

I pray for the safety of mine,

Ours

And yours."

M.R

TIME

"Like most things,

That too, passed."

M.R

FADED

"And even that

Faded

To black."

M.R

THE PAST

"Cry when you're hurt,

Sad,

Or mad.

Cry not,

When what you wanted became,

What you had."

M.R

FREEDOM

"Freedom

Gives you the ability to feel free.

Those things that bind you,

Cast to your feet."

M.R

EAGLE

"Live like an *Eagle*.

Free as a bird."

M.R

SING, GLEAM, BEAM

"Lift every voice and

SING

Let every diamond

GLEAM

I want every heart to

BEAM"

M.R

AFRAID

"Don't be

Afraid

To dive into the open sea,

What if while diving you discover a treasure full of mystery."

M.R

NATURE

"How often do you seek *Nature?*

Only there,

Will you find beauty in its natural

Essence."

M.R

GOOD MUSIC

"There is *Music* in the air,

If you listen for *natures beauty*

There is life in your life,

Believe in what you believe in."

M.R

ANCHORS

"You posses the power to be free.

Break the chain of the *Anchors*

Drowning you at sea."

M.R

NEW PEOPLE

"I love meeting *New People*,

It's a beautiful reminder.

It reminds me how endless life and possibilities are."

M.R

BLINDING LIGHT

"Allow your inner light to shine.

Shine it upon the world,

Those who object will become *Blind*."

M.R

HOPE

"Take each experience

With a grain of salt

And *Hope* for the best.

I sure do

Hope,

A lot."

M.R

INFINITE

"Live with such gentleness,

Equivalent to an infant,

Yet,

Fight with such rage,

One that is

Infinite."

M.R

BELIEVE IN THYSELF

"Believe In ThySelf

Regardless of what they say,

Fight for your cause on any given day."

M.R

DAISY

COFFEE SHOP

I sat alone,

Sipping hot tea

Bright and early,

My favorite *Coffee Shop*

Is my usually.

Usually,

My books and I,

Reading and laughing aloud,

The strangers,

They glance in my direction,

I understand attention.

Insanity accompanies me,

My books are rather interesting.

Alone I sat and there you are,

You smiled at me from across the far.

I blush.

Finding this to be strange

"Daisy."

I imagined you calling my name,

My heart it fluttered even

Skipped beats,

I watched as you occupied the empty seat next to me.

Panicked.

I struggle to pretend you weren't there.

Although,

I'm well aware.

Without any reason,

For an unknown reason I cared

More than I should for a perfect stranger.

I couldn't pretend any longer,

I stand.

Springing up, in a sudden jolt.

I turned away,

Dodging the piercing stare.

"I've done it, almost to the exit."

I thought.

The next sound sunk my heart.

"*Daisy,* You forgot this."

He called out, holding up my book,

I'd overlooked in my escape.

OH, DAISY

Oh, Daisy

You are my world.

Oh, Daisy

What a special girl.

Hey, Daisy

I often think of you.

Oh, Daisy

When you blush

That way,

I know it to be true.

Oh, Daisy

You captivate me.

In a field of daisies you blend beautifully.

Daisy, oh Daisy,

You make my words afraid.

Even when I push them,

I'm unsure of what to say.

Daisy,

My *Daisy,*

How I wish that you knew.

In that same field of beautiful daisies,

I'd forever pick you.

GHOST OF A SMILE

"Tell me you love me."

She whispered hopelessly.

He sat, joining her bedside,

Calmly brushed the hair from her face,

Revealing the most ravishing girl he'd ever known.

She observed closely,

His lips pressed tightly together,

Twitching at the corners,

Concealing an occasional escaping subdued giggle.

The girl studies his every expression,

Confused.

Seconds of silence crept by unnoticed.

Growing self-conscious,

Regretting her decision to be open,

The decision to love,

It was a risk.

Irritated.

After staring into his vacant unfamiliar eyes

And pressed together lips,

Still hiding the faint *Smile*.

"If you don't it's okay."

She said, now defeated,

Not understanding the humor,

She continued.

"Lie to me."

Silence filled the room.

Even the familiar

Ghost Of A Smile,

Vanished.

A single tear escaped,

Catching it midst of its fall,

Wiping the lonely tear away,

Then, taking her by the hand,

Gazing intently into her eyes.

The smile reappeared,

His eyes dazzled green,

The vibrant glow she knew well.

Somewhere in-between the two she felt safe.

"Darling, My darling,

To question my love for you

Is both blasphemy and mockery.

To consider my heart without your beat,

It's impossible, it could not be.

If you consider my love for you as minimal,

You'd be considering wrong.

I survive on thought of loving you.

I am because of you."

She sat blushing,

Struggling to conceal the familiar

Ghost Of A Smile,

Now finding it's way upon her face.

GOODBYE, JUNE

What if you cried

In the midst of *June?*

I wonder if the flowers would

Refuse to bloom?

Or the ocean,

Would it forget to move?

Time

Would it slow?

If you cried,

I assume,

Within a single tear

The world would know.

Does the birds end their magical song for you?

I'm not as delightful,

But, I'd hold your tune.

Oh darling, if you cried,

I'm unsure what I would do.

If you cried,

There certainly wouldn't be a

June.

PERFECT

You are *Perfect*,

Perfect to me.

Your smile resembles sunshine

Well,

At least it does to me.

Your voice brings life to the heart of my city,

The sweetness in your laugh,

That's something I won't be forgetting.

You are always

Perfect,

Again,

Perfect

To me.

9 4

(NINE-FOUR)

SEPTEMBER 4ᵀᴴ

"9 4 Is more than a poetry book, I think of it as a storybook with poetry as the narrator, taking you on thrilling journey. I am inspired by writers, artists, music, people, and everyday life in general. I'd have to say music and my obsession for lyrics and words merged with my love for literature forced this book. 9 4 Is the introduction book for "The StoryBook Series." I thought this was brilliant. Really, It's just a book of inspirations, and thoughts. I wanted to share a piece of me on my birthday, giving birth to (The StoryBook Series)

Happy Birthday Me."

M. RANDALL

94STORYBOOK.COM

INFO@94STORYBOOK.COM

M.R PUBLISHING

M. RANDALL

www.ingramcontent.com/pod-product-compliance
Lightning Source LLC
Chambersburg PA
CBHW070618050426
42450CB00011B/3078